# SHADOWBOXING

Cover Image: David Rathman, Untitled,
ink and watercolor on canvas, 30 x 36 inches, 2009

Cover and interior set in Hypatia Sans Pro and Electra LT Std

Cover and interior design by Gillian Olivia Blythe Hamel

Offset printed in the United States
by Sheridan Books, Chelsea, Michigan
On 55# Glatfelter B19 Antique
Acid Free Archival Quality Recycled Paper

Library of Congress Cataloging-in-Publication Data

Names: Rios, Joseph, author.
Title: Shadowboxing : poems & impersonations / Joseph Rios.
Description: Oakland, California : Omnidawn Publishing, [2017]
Identifiers: LCCN 2017020874 | ISBN 9781632430434
    (softcover : acid-free paper)
Classification: LCC PS3618.I566 A6 2017 | DDC 811/.6–dc23
LC record available at https://lccn.loc.gov/2017020874

Published by Omnidawn Publishing, Oakland, California
www.omnidawn.com    (510) 237-5472    (800) 792-4957
10 9 8 7 6 5 4 3 2
ISBN: 978-1-63243-043-4

# SHADOWBOXING

*poems & impersonations*

JOSEPH RIOS

OMNIDAWN PUBLISHING
OAKLAND, CALIFORNIA
2017

# CONTENTS

It took me a long time (almost two summers and a breakfast) to write the introduction to Joseph Rios' *Shadowboxing: poems & impersonations.* Of course I wanted the shit to come out right, correct, round for round. But there were other elements in the way: relocation, rebirth, and revision. Finally, when I got around to re-reading Rios' book I had the same reaction ("Diablo!") that I had initially when I first read early sections of it almost five years ago, at the VONA/Voices Writing Workshop in Berkeley, CA. I was unequivocally in front of a voice that couldn't be duplicated.

"Voice" and "epic" are words that are distributed loosely in the poetry world. But I use them with all heat that I can muster. Joseph Rios is an original. Only because when you think you have a handle on his work, he moves the target. He does for Xican@ poetics what Jean Toomer's *Cane* did for the Harlem Renaissance: he radicalizes it into an undeniable modernity. And like Toomer, Rios uses all the genres at his disposal. He uses the epistle, the dramatic dialogue, epigrams from popular culture, and even has a Romantic touch.

In the face of erasure, it's all we can do: Write our souls, our lives, our hoods, our dead cars, and our grandmothers into life. My mentor, Raymond R. Patterson, once told me that all the books I was writing were parts of *one* whole book, where the attempt was to write a culture into existence. Rios does this so profoundly in *Shadowboxing.* And the culture is not solely the *hood,* or varying regions in Califas, but revolutionary poetics, fragmented love, memory, ritual, and signifying *toreos.*

Pablo Neruda hoped for a poetry that could feed us with the bounty of bread. Rios' audiences, his *carnales*, want to know if poetry can fix a broken-down Cherokee. That is what the poet, in the shadow of machismo and financial pragmatism, is up against. In "What's the Matter with You," the speaker asks:

*What is revolution*
*anyway?*

Revolution is always in the mix and remix; the electricity of the multitudes, the family, the teachers, all them are surge protectors in Rios' vision. They participate in a collective reading of Rios' portrait of a *poeta* as young brother, fighter, lover, working man:

*You think*
*You original? Please*
*You just*
In the tradition)

...and beyond, I would argue. Rios' identity is transformed into a kaleidoscopic exploration of cultural allusion, folktale, trickster riddles, and lyric poetry. There is no bull's-eye because he keeps moving just when you think it's safe to stand still and aim. There's no easy categorization here—I knew that when I read the required 10 pages of his VONA submission application in 2010.

Oh, and speaking of bulls and bullfighters, I make an embarrassing cameo in *Shadowboxing*. In "Eye of the Tiger, Act V" I ask Joe (Josefo's doppelgänger?) which one is he (bull or bullfighter) and after reading and re-reading *Shadowboxing*, I would argue that Rios is both in all his literary *tercios*, knowing that if he doesn't put himself at risk of getting bloody, then the poems won't be daring (i.e., revolutionary). Ask Chewy, who like Papo in East Harlem, is an archetype of the poet's interlocutor—the real poet in the crew.

*Chewy: Ey puto, I'd make a good character, you should write about me.*
*Josefo: Maybe.*
*Chewy: Don't fuck around. En serio, you gonna write about me?*
*Josefo: I just did.*

Diablo. Then Josefo pulls the curtain down as if he just finished putting us in position to take aim at our hearts.

Willie Perdomo

Exeter, NH

November 2, 2014

# PROLOGUE

**WILLIAM BLAKE:** I cared not for consequences, but wrote.

*Bless the Fathers. Bless the Sons.*
*Bless the Mothers of all sorts.*
*Bless the Jornalero.*
*The Janitor. The Framer.*
*The Plumber. The Mechanic.*
*The Hustler. The Sex Workers.*
*The Thugs. The Jotitos.*
*The Mojaditos.The Spics.*
*Bless the Brown and the Black Beans, too.*
*Bless my Father; Bless his Sons.*
*Forgive his youngest Son,*
*Joseph Adam, for I know*
*exactly what I do.*

\*

First of all, I'm not scared of you mother fuckers. I don't care if you like
anything written here.
(Be real son)
Within each poem, I impersonate many people.
(Be real real son)
I channel them.
[Words are metaphors, Joseph. Signifier-signified relationship, remember?
Weren't you paying attention?]

Yes, every word is an impersonation of the signified, a metaphor. Aristotle,
Borges, Eddie Murphy. That's what I'm doing here, among other things.
This book? Well, it's just an attempt to impersonate myself.

What I write, I write for my best friends, my cousins, old coworkers, my
dead father, and myself. Of my poems, most of you stuffy L.L. Bean-
wearing motha fuckers will probably say:
        "Just a buncha cursing and hiphoppy nonsense." (Wrong.)
        "This young unlearned man's first attempts at the poetically divine

fall harder than Dante's Beelzebub." Lame. (And also, wrong.)
"It's juvenile, uninspired, undeveloped, hodgepodge, messy,
profane, and unoriginal. You see, that's what's wrong with the
educational system today: these kids don't take the craft of writing
seriously." (Wrong.)

[Joseph, I'd like to weigh in on this, if you don't mind.]
Of course.
[Reader, what the young man is getting at here, is an important point.
Unfortunately, the progression of this art form has left some people behind,
families of people, neighborhoods, communities, street corners. With
them, we leave some of the finest spontaneous, organically developed
manipulations, nay, evolutions of language this side of the twentieth and,
yes, twenty-first centuries. Mr. Rios impersonates their heavy referencing,
the attention to sound, rhythm, cadence, word choice, simile, metaphor,
etc. with the same plain speak he knows well—he is introducing the
references his friends/brothers/cousins make all the time to describe the
world around them; he's using the material they employ to qualify the
human experience—he is taking that and introducing it to the rigid forms
of poetry and seeing how they coalesce and how they, most surely, do not.]

Think *Star Wars*, Richard Pryor, *Rocky*, Freddy Fender, Bobby Womack,
Gladys Knight, James Brown, Notorious BIG, Richie Valenzuela, Tower of
Power, and my father in conversation with Gwendolyn Brooks, John Keats,
Oscar Zeta Acosta, and Martin Espada. Think Woody Allen directing *Blood
In, Blood Out*, Philip Levine singing the Isley Brothers, Dick Gregory
dancing Banda. Robert Hass running from La Migra.

My father would have called it "the funk." My older brother might have
called it G-Funk. (They don't know what that is.) Look it up in the
dictionary. Then ask a fourteen-year-old in East Oakland what that means;
they'll tell you. She'll be the one walking to school past the junkies, the
dealers, the pimps. She's never read William Blake because the district
defunded her school's library and added ten-foot iron fences around the
perimeter of the campus.
(Get used to it, son. That's how they treat us.)

Go to Fresno. Go to West Fresno. (*Fresno's Westside was the closest we ever got to the bigtime.*) Go to Parkside. Go to Calwa. Foodtown. Beansville—ask them about it. See, most poor dark people understand this: when they're done taking all your shit, turning off the water, the cable, the lights—when they're done taking you car, your house, your dad, your older brother, and your baby sister, the funk is all you got. It's a way of bobbin and weaving; it's a way of slippin the jab. They can't knock you out if you keep moving.
[Even on the page.]

You don't understand. They're killing us off one by one. We're being systematically annihilated, destroyed, dismembered, eliminated, exterminated, deported, executed, and incarcerated. I've been around, you know. I've seen this shit. I'm talking about boys, young boys, smaller than these, younger than these hauled off in chains, gunned up and clapped quick, shanked up. They're all wet.

[Joseph, please explain.] Explain what? I'm in my zone right now.
[Please, explain what you mean by "wet," so they all can understand.]

Damn, man. Are you serious? First of all, if Nabokov decides to use French or Russian in his English work, we are all supposed to fall in line and either A: Skip over what we don't know or B: Learn French and Russian. But the second a brotha like myself decides to use slang, in Spanish or English or both, I gotta follow up and tell you what I *really* mean—gotta hold a motha fucka's hand and shit. Look, when someone says, "Ima get you all wet, bruh." That means they're going to puncture your skin with a bullet or something sharp enough to spread your insides all over the pavement and get your clothing *wet* with your own blood. There, you happy now? Is that clear enough? Can I continue? [Yes, thank you.]

Where was I ? Oh yeah. Maybe this is a good time to explain the phrase: "He Go." This phrase defines my poetics. "Go" is not a verb here, but rather, an adjective in the progressive tense. It's like the person is in constant motion. He/she embodies forward motion. (Can't stop, won't stop.)

While walking down the street with a homie of mine, a stranger
commented on his pants: "Them pants too tight for you, patna." Then
his boy said, "Nah, leave the brotha alone. He go." To this, the dude
responded,
"Nah, you got it wrong, playa—He *went*."

This spontaneous manipulation of a manipulation is the sort of linguistic
magic that happens on the street everyday. People are inventing and adding
to the language. Not only was my homie "go-ing," but he'd already been
there.
(They listenin, but they aint hearin you. Say it again.)
I said, not only was he going, he'd already been there.

Whatever. I don't need your approval or your praise. If this racket doesn't
work out, I can always go back to mowing lawns/working on cars/working
on airplanes, etc. I'll be fine. I know my poetry go. My poetry went. It's
done that, and already been there. It's gone. You can't even find it. Shit,
that's not even what's important here.

Want to impress me? Get a Dream Act passed with no military option.
Support literacy in every hood and hamlet. Teach Hamlet in every hood.
Get more healthy produce to Huntington Park. Fund libraries and
good teachers. Stop banning books that make brown people proud of
themselves. Support the Third World College. Buy art. Pay artists. Explain
the historical significance of my father's curly hair. Cure the cancer in
my Grandfather's kidney, in my Mother's breast, in my Tia's lungs and
ovaries. Bring back my Tia Cookie. Bring back Cissie and Michele. Stop
letting pesticides into the water. Stop deporting mothers. Stop incarcerating
fathers and sons. Let boys be girls and girls be boys. And when all else fails,
imitate Zapata and Shakespeare. c/s

Joseph Rios
Fresno
11 January 2012

P.S.: If you don't like the phrase *mother fucker*, I suggest you put the book down and go get lost in IKEA. I say fuck at least a hundred times a day to keep my teeth white—that's way less than David Mamet used in *Glengarry Glen Ross* and they gave that guy the Pulitzer.

# ROUND ONE: DING DING

**ROCKY:** You gotta be a moron... you know what I mean? It's the only racket where you're almost guaranteed to end up a bum.

*ACT I, SCENE 1*

*SEMITRUCK. CIGARETTES. TALK RADIO.*
*JERKING TRANSMISSION. LA VIRGEN DE*
*GUADALUPE. FRESNO IS IN THE MIDDLE OF*
*EVERYWHERE.*

*LARRY LEVIS: Still, even when they laughed, they laughed in Spanish.*

CHEWY: So you go to school n shit, huh?

JOSEFO: Yeah.

CHEWY: Whatchu wanna do with that?

JOSEFO: I wanna be a writer.

CHEWY: No mámes. And write about what?

JOSEFO: I don't know. Whatever, foo.

CHEWY: You make good money doin' that?

JOSEFO: Nah. Not really.

CHEWY: So why the hell you do it?

JOSEFO: Fuck if I know.

CHEWY: You probably do it for the pussy. Don't lie, fucker.

JOSEFO: Man, just drive the fuckin' truck.

CHEWY: No mámes. I knew it.

JOSEFO: Fuckouttahere.

CHEWY: You gonna write about me?

JOSEFO: Fuck you.

CHEWY: Ey puto, I'd make a good character. You should write about me.

JOSEFO: Maybe.

CHEWY: Don't fuck around. En serio, you gonna write about me?

JOSEFO: I just did.

*Curtain.*

# SOUTHPAW CURSE

*For Ramiro & Victor Martinez*

**I**

To begin:
Fresno y tambien un fresno
weeping a stench of ash
exhausted by fumes & cut grass
you can't smell from the I-5

Look beyond Arax's tales at the thumb
pressed firmly upon two pruning arms
tearing through the sinuous shoulders
of smoking palm fronds you mistake for Fire-
baugh Mendota or maybe Kerman

*Later*

*The spilled milk sours when*
*Little Josefo's hands return from the hoe*
*with callouses of brown skin*
*hardened over bloody soil*
*just like the lunar on Tia's face*

## II

The Parrot still migrates
with the geese along the old
Golden State toward the water
treatment plant on Jensen

Knobs of aborted bulbs
form praying fingers
instead of irises

Delfino trims his nails
against the fan blade
of his work truck

The wailing escapes
through broken windows
into a horror of muted dust
5W-30 and light


*Later*

*Ramiro parks his elliptical bike in Tokyo*
*Garden goes inside and drinks two bottles*

*of warm sake and reads* Parrot in the Oven
*in the voice of Burgess Meredith*

*His mouth labors over words*
*like* tomato *and* lightning

*He leaves rubbing his throat*
*still with much more to say*

23

## III

An airplane drops a white
cloud upon brown bodies

Powder sifts gently
onto eyebrows
wrists and shoelaces

Mother instructs small children
to hide under vines

The good ones die before forty
The rest of us wake up
with swollen feet and nosebleeds


*Later*

*Josefo kicks an empty bottle*
*across the alley then vomits*

*beneath a honey bee*
*with four sagging breasts*

*Ramiro searches for eloi*
*above scaffolding at Broadway*

*Victor appears behind the orange*
*glow of an American Spirit*

*A police siren screams again*
*again & again*
*Does no one else hear that?*

## IV

The Central Valley is an aging
fruit tree breaking concrete
with the knuckles of its toes

The sidewalks stay warm
under naked feet slapping
from one street lamp to the next

The Parrot places his head
in the oven to escape the cancer
hiding in every breath

When eulogized the priest
will mistake this for mercy


*Later*

*Carved letters appear*
*on an ash tree that must*

*outgrow its ambivalence*
*The letters read:*

I am the American, güey

# * ADDENDUM:

Some years ago, a student at City College rented space at Broadway Studios in Downtown Fresno. There, the student met Ramiro—noted painter, muralist, philosopher, and brother to the poet Victor Martinez. One late evening in the studio, Victor came to visit. Miro made the introduction:

"Hey, Vic, meet my friend. He writes poems, too."

The three men walked to a nearby liquor store and bought thirty-two ounce bottles of Bud Ice. Somewhere on the Fulton Mall, a street couple argued in an empty fountain. When the three finished the first round, they walked back to the liquor store and bought more. They enacted this ritual several times before the night's end. The student paid close attention, laughed, and contributed when able.

Miro liked talking about the look of the San Joaquin river before the dams and canals—the wildlife, the marsh land, the tabletop mountains, the sea shells still coating the valley floor. Victor spoke very little throughout the night. But everything he said was in a low glasspack tenor—like a work truck idling in an oil-spotted driveway, puffing out rhythmic clouds of exhaust into the cold morning air.

The student passed out on a spinning couch chair in the hallway between a row of closed studio spaces. The Martinez men skipped out. Their voices and laughter echoed off the brick warehouse walls. The wrought iron door slammed hard behind them, vibrating loudly at first, then softly in its jamb. One year later, Victor was dead.

# THINK ABOUT THE FIGHT

This is the sum of many Sundays
And Eighteen Art Laboe dedications
Never aired in towns called Wasco
Coalinga Sanger McFarland & Fowler
Where we're taught to be negatively capable
Criminal Kil[liminal] Eye tee why

> *Neither One of Us Ready To Die*
> *Suevecito Gladys Bootsy*
> *War Lighter Shade of*
> *Say It Loud*
> *I'm Brown & I'm Proud*

Ask around
(I'm a crate diver's dream)

　　　　[In this place discovery of source
　　　　　　　prefaces all understanding]

And besides
　　　(Chitlin' blues
　　　　　Women have all the answers)

My brother　　His open window　　The cold

highway ninetynine　　Pink oleander bushes

clipped at the knuckle　　Dried　　Blown

Raked　　　swiftly into thirty-two-gallon buckets

Tossed over shoulders    into trailer    Stomped

under jagged Timbs We must believe the cholo

version of Rapper's Delight still exists in Dad's

two-door Honda Accord    Wherever that may be

*PAULIE: He can't train to the jungle junk music.*
*You can't train him like a coloured fighter. He ain't got no rhythm.*

(I'm sentimental

You know why?

Cuz the people        sentimental

Watch me
I feel like

Movin

I wanna          Move

I got ta                    Move

Move

I gotta                Move On

Move          Move    on          Move on up

I got ta      Get on up                    Get on Up

Got  ta                    Get  back Get Back      Get ta      steppin

Got ta            Get Right            Get Straight

Get on up      I gotta  Get on Up      I gotta  Get Down          I gotta

Get by                      That's the way

That's the way                    We get by                    Way
we get by

[It's so hard
to say good

It's just
So damn hard

To say) -bye]
By n by

[ Think Humphrey Bogart. Woody Allen
  performed this creative exercise in *Play it
  Again, Sam.* Oscar Zeta Acosta did this, too,
  but found less fanfare. The author asks you to
  consider a concept captured in a well-known
  Broadway musical. They called it: *Tradition.* ]

(Woody Allen tho? For real?)

[ The author understands that Sylvester Stallone
  is much more Brando than Bogey and *Rocky*
  is much more *On the Waterfront* than, say, *The
  Maltese Falcon.* And if specificity is what you
  desire, Rocky's yelling of the name "Adrian"
  does recall Brando's "Stella!" in *Streetcar
  Named Desire.* The author intended to
  compose something of a juxtaposition...]

(Alright, we get it. Daym.)

[If you seek a more direct source for the Bogart
  reference, read Andre Bazin's "The Death of
  Humphrey Bogart."]

(I said, we get it, Mr. Peabody.)

[Well, now you know.]

(Chitlins are nothin' but tripas to me
        Look I'm teaching you how
        to walk son Keep your eyes on
        me if you know whats good
        What it is What it do
        What? You jivin' me?
        I know you ain't jivin'
        me boy I didn't raise no
        chicken shit
        jive turkey motha
        fucka motha fucka Nah
        you listenin'
        butchu ain't hearing me
        You lookin' at the originator
        of this game OG mack
        paht nuh You think
        you original? Please
        You just
        *In the tradition*)

## II

(Don't get hostile now
      Understand It's simple
      mathematics What's yours is mine
      And what's mine is
      mine Without me you ain't
      shit I maydju

      You minus me
      Ain't    Shit
      Huh?
      Yeah   I maydju
      New Years Eve
      I maydju drunk
      as shit humpin
      all      Up
      on that mama
      of yours      I maydju

      I maydju

      Understand?
      I maydju
      With this)

      Yes
      With This
      And more importantly

But uh,
back to the lecture
at hand.

See, that's where we keep
our most cherished
booty and Tina she got a biggo...


(But, What's Love
            Got to do
            Go to do with it?)

[Biggie variation omitted.]

What is revolution anyway?
but Table Slapping
Plain talk Ab-surd
Shameless Q-Tip
Syllabic Em pha sis

            [No relation to Mike Myers
                        or films about flight attendants.]


(The Technics son. Tell 'em about the Technics.)


            Just spin the motherfucker, I said.
            Tear the knobs from doors &
            consider the etymology
            with open, spread
            ringless fingers.

What becomes of me
        After that day passes &
We of the lighter &
        Darker shades of Brown
End wars
        Over territory
Un incorporated?

When we
        Remove saddles
From backs

And say first
        and irrevocably
We belong here, dammit.

# THEY DONT REMEMBER YOU;
# THEY REMEMBER THE REP

*ACT I, SCENE 2*

*BUBBY. RUDE. CADDY. KINGS. BROTHA LYNCH.*
*EASTSIDE. BLUNTS. BAG OF SHAKE. VELVET.*
*LOTS OF IT.*

BUBBY: So your daddy bought you that new Street Fighter huh?

JOSEFO: Yeah, it's cool.

BUBBY: When we get back, I'ma beat your ass like a lil bitch.

RUDE: Bubby, come on man.

BUBBY: I'm just fuckin with the kid. (Laughs)

He's got nothing on my yoga fire. (Reenacts motion)

Hey there goes that buster right now!

RUDE: Benny?

BUBBY: Yeah man! I swear to fuckin God!

RUDE: Go back.

BUBBY: That dude's twice your size!

RUDE: I got something for his big ass. Hey Jojo, grab me that bat. It's by your feet.

JOSEFO: But that's my bat.

BUBBY: We're gonna give it back. Don't trip.

RUDE: Don't get too close, Bub. Right here.

BUBBY: I knew this was gonna be a good day.

RUDE: Stop here, Bubby. Let's go.

JOSEFO: Rudy, what about me?

BUBBY: Ah fuck, come on man.

RUDE: [To BUBBY] Hold up.

    [To JOSEFO] You're gonna stay here, Jojo. Keep your head down. This shit is not for you.

*Curtain.*

# ARS POETICA, THREE GENERATIONS

*CLOVIS, CA*

Seventy years later a great grandson called Josefo built a treehouse
on the corner of 8th and DeWitt. He laid three two-by-four arms
across branches and hammered a wide piece of plywood to make
a floor. When he finished, he sprawled across the board and fell
asleep. In his sleep, he rolled off the platform. For a moment, he
saw the branches going by him on all sides. The few noteworthy
events of his life did not suddenly flash through his mind. This was
not a dream. Josefo collided with a limb and tumbled to the grass
below. The fall knocked the wind out of him. He laid there gasping
on the lawn. No one saw him and no one could hear him. When
he regained his breath, he got up and climbed back into the tree.
To Josefo, this history is common knowledge. If you asked him, he
would tell you. But you wouldn't believe him.

# ROUND TWO: SAVING NATIONS

**APOLLO:** Damn man! What the hell you doin? This man will knock you on your ass! You thought I was tough? This chump will kill yah. Come on! What's the matter with you?

**ROCKY:** Tomorrow. Let's do it tomorrow.

Josefo's college roommate once believed it necessary to take over Wheeler Hall at Berkeley, chain the doors, and hold off the police for many days. There are many well-recorded facts that could have motivated such an action. When asked to explain himself, his roommate recited this Mario Savio line from memory:

*There comes a time when the operation of the machine becomes so odious, makes you so sick at heart, that you can't take part, you can't even passively take part and you've got to put your bodies upon the gears and upon the wheels, upon all the apparatus, and you've got to make it stop*

Ishmael Armendariz, known to his Grandmother and only his Grandmother as *Ismael*, explained the need for direct action in this manner. Commenting further, Ish went on to recall Tupac's famous poetic metaphor of the rose that grew from concrete. Ishmael said that we should encourage and foster the growth of these roses, yes, but that this was not enough. The problem lies not with the roses, no, the problem is one of concrete. Ishmael said:

*We roses have to do more than show off our pretty petals. We roses must grow hands and feet. We roses must remove the concrete, man, or none this shit is worth a damn.*

(Foo, dontchuknow
Revolution is just Romance?)
Martin Espada wrote something
about a lover's hands
Circling Grasping Clasping
(Huggin n Shit) Tellin Me
You know nothing of love
I asked instead for a bus pass
Like a smart ass on his way to mass
Not a donkey, but the thing we carry behind us


*Dear Professor Marcial Gonzalez,*

> *I hate to be the one to deliver this message*
> *But the poet known as Luis Omar Salinas*
> *Also known as: The Crazy Gypsy*
> *Also known as: Salinas*
> *Also known as: The Aztec Angel*
> *Also known as: Omar*
>
> *Died while performing the Salinas Shuffle*
> *He will not be available for a reading now or*
> *In the future*
>
> *Javier and I wanted to buy a photo*
> *of him and Jose Montoya*
> *the grandfather of us all*
> *but we couldn't afford*
> *the $100 price tag      Oh yeah*
> *I'm still wrestling with your section on*
> *The Parataxis-Hypotaxis Antinomy*

*Honestly     parts of it are still too much*
*for a dirty-faced mocoso like me but*
*something about it makes a lotta sense*


*Abrazo,*
*JR*

Meanwhile
Back at the ranch:

Billie Dee sellin malt liquor
The Beave huffin
Through a Che tshirt
Mexicanitos multiply
In third grade classrooms
& Freddy Soto's still dead
          Regardless

Richmond Amtrak
Thinking on Calwa
Grandma's bobby pins
Hoodied passengers
Rockyesque docks
Barbed wire grays
Endor Walkers*

          *See the sea*
                    *Needs protection*
                    *From the nakedness*
                    *Of your brown toes*

Itchy chin hair
Bald head no beanie
Words like Justice
& Stylistic in all of it
Gimme a bigote
For all seasons
Like Coppolla
Samuel Beam

Furious Styles
Fidel Castro
Monk &
Common Sense

## * CORRECTION:

Recently Josefo was made aware of a gross error in his referencing. While reading an early draft of this poem at their grandmother's house, his cousin, a superior *Star Wars* fan, pointed out that the Walkers most resembling the Oakland cranes were never on Endor. In fact, the walkers that appear on the forest moon in *Return of the Jedi* were much smaller. Josefo hoped to reference the All Terrain Armored Transport (AT-AT) walkers, also known as the Imperial Walkers, famed for their contribution to the Rebel Alliance's defeat at the Battle of Hoth during the Galactic Civil War.

George Lucas says he did not model their design after the dock cranes set about the Oakland coastline, but George Lucas is full of shit. Everyone knows this. The author thanks Gabriel Pacheco for this correction.

*ACT II, SCENE 1*

*ALFRED. BARROWS HALL. UNIVERSITY OF CALIFORNIA.*

ARTEAGA: The xicano is the subject of Aztlan the cultural nation
        but not the state and not subject to capricious borderlines.
        It is not a state of being but rather an act, *xicando*, the
        progressive tense, *ando xicando*, actively articulating
        self. The infinitive *xicar* meaning to play, to conflict, to work
        out dialogically unfinalized versions of self. Yes, Josefo?
JOSEFO: Profe, how does this relate to our poetry?
ARTEAGA: Josefo, you must understand this if you are to have
        even the most elementary understanding of our poetics.
JOSEFO. Are there any books on Xicano/a Poetics?
ARTEAGA: Yes, but only one.
JOSEFO: Who wrote it?
ARTEAGA: Me.
*Curtain.*

*BERKELEY, CA*

Josefo was hiding in the restroom, again. He heard two come in. One of them was telling the other a story in Spanish. Something another guy told him in front of the bookstore. They were laughing on the outside because there were no white people around. Josefo heard one of them whip open a plastic garbage bag. He flushed the toilet even though he hadn't used it. He picked up his backpack. One of the men left as he came out of the stall. Josefo walked over to the sink and robotically washed his hands. The man's face was pointed downward and toward the trash can. Josefo looked at his hands. He shut off the water. The man hadn't refilled the paper towels. Josefo used his shirt. He walked past the man and mumbled something between, *Con permiso* and *Excuse me*. The man didn't look up at him. This was the furthest Josefo had ever been from home.

Outside it was still raining. Josefo stopped in the middle of the passing crowd and looked up at the Campanile ringing over Berkeley. Someone bumped into him. Then another. And another. And an other.

Night. Josefo is drunk, stumbling down the sidewalk. POV shot of him walking, mumbling. He tries to get into Nene's apartment complex. The door is locked. He walks down to the gate, the disabled access gate. He yanks the gate and its hydraulic arm open. He runs up the steps and then down one flight. He falls into a puddle. He gets up. He rings the doorbell. No answer. He calls her cell. Still, nothing.

Josefo pees in some bushes in front of her apartment. He climbs onto some railing, then clings to electrical piping that's been bracketed to the wall. He makes it high enough so that her third floor window can be reached with an outstretched broom. He extends and slaps the bristles against her pane. He loses his balance and leaps away from the wall, landing hard on his feet and ankles. He tumbles on the wet grass. There he stays, falls asleep. He wakes up some time later wet and smelling of his own vomit.

Josefo walks back to the front door. He rings the doorbell. Still, nothing. He calls her phone, again. He can hear it ringing through the open window. He yells to her. She wakes. She yells at him. She leaves her room to open the door. The two of them walk up the steps to the bathroom. They undress and enter the shower. She washes him. Josefo washes her breasts. He lathers them over and over, carefully.

Nene falls back onto the bed. Josefo picks up one of the books on the table and flips through it [*Bloodroot*, Alma Luz Villanueva]. Nene falls asleep. He continues to read. Room is dark. The record player spins, but we can only hear the hum of the needle cutting over blank wax. A soft lamp warms his shoulder, his lap, but things are still difficult to see. Josefo is awake and staring at Nene while she sleeps. Eventually he falls asleep. Nene opens her eyes, much later, as if from a dream. Lamp's off. Josefo is not moving. His body is a mass of shadow and moonlight coming through the open window and onto her dorm style bed. She stares a while to confirm he is breathing; he is still alive. Josefo's shoulder rises. Josefo is still breathing. He's breathing, snoring now from the throat. Like a growl, she thinks. She puts her head down and drapes her leg over his body.

The next morning, Josefo found Nene on the couch. He stepped over a puddle on the floor and noticed the bruises on each shoulder. Sitting upright, she began telling a story about a six-foot, two-inch, two-hundred-and-fifty-pound beast, how he awoke during the night swinging fists, arms, and face—how he relieved himself there in the hallway. She gave time to the careful explanation of the beast's hands, how large, how much larger in the dark, how unfamiliar the grip of each flexing digit, how each finger conspired against the flesh of her arms, how unfamiliar the beast's voice asking, terrified: *Who are you?*

Concrete. Fist. Knuckle. Bone. Sheetrock. Powder. Bob. Weave. Nail. Stud. Swing. Boxers. Hands. Jaw. Head. Bob. Weave. Thread. Stitch. Mother. Father. Meat. Flesh. Kittens. Bodies. Head. Tail. Paw. Scattered. Slip. Jab. Sweep. Broom. Trash. Hide. Bury. Shovel. Pick. Swing.

"Who are you?" she asked. "Who are you when you go to sleep? Who are you when you lay down in that dark? When the shadows creep over our blankets—Who are you then? Who gave me these bruises? Who pissed on the floor? Who were you shouting at? Who were you swinging at?"

*ACT II, SCENE 2*

*ERIC. BACKYARD. BEERCANS. CHIHUAHAS.*
*CARLOS DIGGING A HOLE FOR THE BIRRIA.*
*TIAS EVERYWHERE DOING WHATEVER TIAS DO.*

JOE: Yo, so there's this poet right.

ERIC: A what?

JOE: A poet, fucker. His name was Czeslaw Milosz.

ERIC: Hey check those jackstands. I don't want this jeep fallin on
       my ass.

JOE: They're on there. Hey, I'm tryna tell you some real shit here.

ERIC: Lift it higher. Up. Up. There.

JOE: So this dude's a badass poet. Got awards and everything.

ERIC: You still on that tip?

JOE: Fuck, man. Hear me out.

ERIC: Fine. Go 'head. And get me that box of hardware over there.

JOE: Here. So anyway, he wrote, "What is poetry that doesn't save
       nations and people?"

ERIC: What?

JOE: What is poetry that doesn't save nations and people?

ERIC: What?

JOE: What is poetry that doesn't save nations and people?! You deaf?

ERIC: Well, shit, I had the compressor on.

JOE: Did you listen to me, bitch?

ERIC: I heard you. So tell me something Mr. Nations and People...

JOE: What?

ERIC: Can any of those poems save the fuckin' Cherokee?

*Curtain.*

# ADVICE

PETE MAYORGA: *First thing, get rid of this Cherokee shit.*
*Second thing: getchu a Yota from the early 90s.*
*Make sure it's 4x4 with a manual shift.*
*Pay a mad genius with a wrench to play with the gears.*
*The trick is, you wanna slow this mother fucker down.*
*You want the son of a bitch to crawl slow and powerful.*
*Click. Click. Flex over every dimple in the trail.*
*Speed is your enemy. That's how you get fucked up.*
*Do I need to explain torque to you again?*

*Listen, drive up to the Sierras below Yosemite. You know the place.*
*Take some fuckers as crazy as you, a lotta food, a lotta beer*
*and a lotta ammunition. But none of that dueling banjos shit*
*even though you'd probably like that you hippie mother fucker.*
*Oh hey, and one last thing: put some fuckin shoes on,*
*you crazy bastard. Who do you think you are, Huck Finn?*

# ROUND THREE: ROPE A DOPE

**MICKEY:** If you ever get hurt and you feel that you're goin' down, this little angel is gonna whisper in your ear. It's gonna say, "Get up you son of a bitch, because Mickey loves yah."

Before first light, nine men, mostly tradesmen, in exactly six trucks drove up to Fresno Dome. They brought beer and meat. They departed caravan-style up the 41 freeway. They found snow and ice near Bass Lake. By 11 a.m., the men were drunk and wandering the forest, looking for wood. The trucks traveled in pairs. Abel, the craziest dude in the crew, took the two youngest with him. "You two homos come with me," he said. "Bring your ice chest."

Once parked, Abel pulled out his rifles and ammunition: thirty aught six and a .22 for each of the youngsters. "Shoot the tip of that tree over there," Abel said. "Like this." Abel leaned his wide upper body onto the bed of his truck and took a wide triangular stance for balance. He turned his ball cap around and closed one eye. The first shot rang out and echoed off the trees. "Money shot, baby," he said. Soon, the three were taking aim and firing on the sapling fifty yards away, slowly clipping the trunk from top to bottom. The farther down the trunk they got, the more bullets it took to make it bend over. At the middle, they expended casing after casing. A small pile of brass accumulated at their feet, mixed with larger beer cans. But the sapling refused to bend over. Frustrated, Abel yelled for the boys to stop shooting. "Cease fire! Cease fire, motha fuckers!" he yelled. "I said cease fire, goddammit!" The youngsters put their weapons down. The shoeless one popped open a fresh beer and took a long swig.

Abel walked into the line of fire. "Watch this," he said. Twenty
yards from the sapling, Abel reached into his left armpit and pulled
out a three fifty-seven magnum and pointed the barrel forward
and squeezed the trigger, still walking toward the tree. With
his shoulders square over firmly placed steps, he smoothly and
deliberately pulled the trigger. Hammer back, pull, bang! Hammer
back, pull, pow! "Fuck you, mother fucker!" Hammer back, pull,
boom! "Bang, bang, bitch! You like that?! You like that?!" After six
shots, the tree finally bent over. Abel emptied the casings onto the
forest floor, reloaded, and holstered the hand cannon under his arm.
"Now that's how it's done!" he said. "One of you pussies owes me a beer."

Block rubber truck tires
lose traction in wet mud.
One forgets to turn with or against.
You should know: lipped cigarettes
protract, too, in times of great peril.

> [What good is a man if he cannot articulate
> the muddy crevices of a forest trail?]

This always ends with what's left of a felled tree.
Read a friend's story about summer dresses
and the foreign exchange* student just out
of reach far away and blurred filled in and recreated
with attempted replacement.

> [Likewise, what good is a man who knows not
> how to tie a dignified knot?]

Josefo walked around the lot at Madera Wine.
The coughing tractor inhaled the gray cloud
hovering over the vines. He forgot
about his dangling laces and fell
face first into a puddle.

*

This is not a reference to the hip hop crew
known as "The Foreign Exchange."

Someday soon, Joseph Marcure
will write his masterpiece
Listen to him typing away
with Mom
with Matt
with dog
with cats
and unsent letters to
Dennis Cooper.

You have no idea
how good it can get.

The poor and hungry make line,
        wait for their portion of bread
        and holy Neutral Milk.

Think On These Things:
Tennies, twirling shoe string, leave your tennies, the bottle, the
panties, Sanger, concrete, concrete canal, crooked nails, iron rust,
tree trunk, tire swing, take a swig, cigarettes, perky titties, heavenly
nipples, smirking glances, fingers in your pockets, the dry fields, your
erection, the sunset, her sandy toes, your sperm in the water, the
rows of muscat, tied vines, wire cutters, thick-knuckled fingers, the
outline of her wet body stamped on the passenger seat of your Jeep.

# TWO JOSEFOS

## I

The boy down the street smells
like peepee and his pants don't fit.
He fell off his bike one day
and had no one to watch him cry.

When you step off the back porch,
your hands full of garbage,
you can hear Abuelo's cracked head
swell up and pop like chewing gum.
All this, before they sliced you
from my mother. You never met him.

Something's burning in the house.
Could be Tío's beard. The hallways
smell of tortillas made a mano.
Mom got used to the beating
of the rolling pin knocking
repeatedly like the revolving
hand on the kitchen clock
thrust into the dough, kneading,
clenching fists, holding
tightly onto yesterday's flour.

No one move. Can you hear it?
The rolling pin. Knocking.
Abuelo's head on the concrete.
Knocked out cold one last time.

## II

Two Josefos took one class at city college
Two Josefos celebrated over gin and Eazy-E
Two Josefos called one Nene
Two Josefos walked 14 blocks
Two Josefos woke one angry father

One Nene drove up to the sidewalk
One Nene said get the fuck in the car
One Nene yelled at two Josefos
One Nene is sick and fuckin tired
One Nene doesn't have to deal with this shit
Two Josefos are ridiculous
Two Josefos should get some fuckin help
One Nene left two Josefos at the bus stop

Two Josefos went Nay Nay Nay
all the way home

*ACT III, SCENE 1*

*FARMHOUSE BACKYARD. DITCH WITCH.*
*NEW LANDSCAPE. TRENCHING FOR WELL*
*WATER. SUMMER. THIRTEEN. NO SHADE.*
*DELANO IS ON THE ROAD TO DAMASCUS.*

DAD: Whoa! Shut it down!

JOSEFO: (Turning off the machine) What happened?

DAD: Do you see what you're doing?

JOSEFO: Yeah, I'm digging the trench just like you said.

DAD: No, you're not. Look at what you're doing.

JOSEFO: Yeah, there's a trench from the well all the way over here.
    And?

DAD: You don't see what you're doing, do you?

JOSEFO: It's right there, oldman. Just like you said.

DAD: Put your hand out and look in front of you. Do any of your
    lines look straight?

JOSEFO: They're straight enough.

DAD: Son, what did I tell you? You have to hold on tight to this
    machine or it'll get away from you. You can't let it get away
    from you. You gotta correct it along the way or you'll go
    awry the way you've done here.

JOSEFO: I did it the way you showed me.

DAD: Stick your hand out there again. Look at the lines you've
    made.

JOSEFO: What for?

DAD: Do it, son. Put your hand out there. Look at what you've made
    here. You haven't been doing this as long as me. And you

are going to go awry sometimes. If these were my lines, they would zigzag from edge to edge.

JOSEFO: Fine, I'll fix it.

DAD: Stop. Listen to what I'm saying. I need you to hear me right now. I have to go to the other worksite. When I leave, I'm not going to be here to watch you. You'll be here by yourself, understand? I need you to start again at the well and re-dig this trench. This time, do it the way I taught you, Son, not the way I showed you. You get me?

JOSEFO: Yes, Dad.

*Curtain.*

# MOONFLOWER

Outside, Josefo drags a swisher &
two tall boys behind the garage
Grandpa built three decades ago.
The view is better and he can't be seen.

*El Nieto is a recovering chauvinist and*
*a habitual gardener*
*who recites poems to tomatoes*
*rotting green-red in water.*

*Asi se hace mas indio,*
*mas feo, mas chango,*
*mas chango, mas feo feo.*

[ Retreat from white rays inaudible
into the shadow of woven straw and
think romantically of the night. Hold
onto the memory of your own voice and
ask like-minded questions while pacing:
Inhale, then exhale. ]

Aside:

Once a month we lovers
celebrate the period with dark
towels spread over white sheets

Our love is a game of pretend oft played
on the warm cement of the driveway
under your father's Volvo station wagon

*

When it happened,
the unpacked bags
said nothing about it.
Notepad, this name,
cursive, clean sheet,
lined paper, block letters.
Nene tore the page out
wadded it into a ball
and threw it as hard
as she could.

Later, the red skirt that rides
up her ass and she knows it. Oh,
and a promise. You know the one:
   *I swear to God.* Drink enough, fuck
a stranger


*Later*

*Texting nonsense. Humming.*
*One more beer. Urine in an open field of grain.*
*Sanger. Del Rey. Reedley. You can't be sure.*
*There's a cow forty yards out that you can't see.*
*Falling asleep there in the truck bed under a moving*
*blanket becomes the lesser of most any evil.*

# NO PAIN

For to Adelante:
In case of an emergency,
crush aforementioned glass
and resurrect Andres Montoya,
fallen Prince of Locura; cura.

After a forced entry,
they found flour tortillas,
Freddy Fender & Gertrude Stein's
inspiration of Luther Vandross:

A chair is still.
A room is still &
you are never the only vato.

*

Arthritic and crippled, abuelas still die
of lung diseases language refuses to impersonate.
Repollo me dijó así: Los canciónes de Doña Helen
never turn to vinegar. We can hear them
repeated in the furrows and files where we tear
sheets of foil from our cold pig parts,
our tomato bouillon, our fried egg,
our cactus cubes, our diabetes medicines.
One bit shared each to each, as each are worth.
The teenager among us sits to one side
under the cover of some vines. He's been
quiet all morning. He mouths along
with poems set to music. Each bar enters
his ear through a pair of foam headphones.

Josefo found the funeral photo in one piece; in it, the boy's looking
at several fated photos with a smile over Paul, dead, wearing the
alderman's windsor knot that mourning fixed into a frowning
triangle and cinched to the base of a developing lump; flout now at
this juvenile mouth of mettle and wire; pay heed to father's epistle
to the Filipinos; his creeping saliva beat down with fists and these
clasping fingers, tearing down, tearing up, thrusting into another,
its twin; four fingers, clasped, tearing, adding frayed white edges
to glossy fragments of gelled hair and a Southern Baptist foyer,
mumbling four letter words filtered through lips clasped, crying,
finally, like a little bitch in Nana's unkempt garage.

# THE SIXTEENTH ROUND

**ADRIAN:** It doesn't matter what I believe, because you're the one that's gotta carry that fear around inside you. Afraid that everybody's gonna take things away, afraid you're gonna be remembered as a coward, and that you're not a man anymore...

## TO: DOÑA SERROS
## FROM: BESPECTACLED JOVEN

*For Michele Serros (1966 – 2015)*

This could have been an ode
to your fur coat, to your gold shoes
stuck in the mud outside Salinas,
to tilled acres, to grandmothers
that live in the house, to poets
reading poems at Lollapalooza,
to cassettes and cassette tape
iphone cases, to water tower
selfies in strange front yards,
to wide-laced hats, comadre-
only tea times, vegan tamales,
50-year-old quinceñeras and
East LA punk bands named
Edward James Olmos.

Begging your pardon, Dona,
your Joven should be writing
an ode to the bullhorn
you used at the gallery
en La Mision, San Pancho.
I should be writing an ode
to La Mickey, La Giggles, and
La Chicana Falsa's whispers
extinguishing sound from lips,
an ode to whispers fishing laughs
from bellies, whispers draining
eyes of their tears, whispers
lifting asses from seats,
some loud ass street dude
making a mess in aisle five,
fierce incantatory whispers
pulling hands into other hands
clap clap clapclap clapping,

more tears, an ode to tears,
an ode to laughter, an ode
to Tias who said you'd never
become a writer, nunca.

And that moon? That moon
over 24<sup>th</sup> Street just as loud
as gold shoes in the mud,
loud as wide-laced hats,
loud as a fake fur coat,
loud as candle flames
on a dark night in Berkeley.
Dark like the night you left.
An ode to the darkness
for making us see
that moon, those candles,
an ode to Celia's prayer,
to Ester's bracelets lifted
in the air, an ode to
holding hands
in bedroom, in living room,
down steps, floating,
more tears, floating
over neighbor's
tossed white petals,
that candlelight again,
that moon again, floating
into the big limousine.
Do you remember, Doña?
Do you remember how
the moon came to see
you off? Down Ashby,
Adeline, Broadway
to Oxnard,
to Oxnard.
I should be writing
an ode to the sea
in Oxnard,

in Oxnard.
And I know you left us
on a skateboard
sneaker kicked, pushed
over fresh streets
swerving
under bent knees
around the cliffs
on the 101,
your hand,
your fingers
waving in the breeze
to the waves,
to the sand,
to the sun,
to the fields,
and all those
pretty goddamned
things.
I should be writing
an ode to your fingers.
Don't leave, Doña.
Your fingers.
You're still
kicking,
you're still
pushing, gliding.
Your fingers
gently brush
the repeating
yellow lines
on the road: gone.

CAR SPEAKERS:

| | |
|---|---|
| *The Town I Live In Is Lonely* | Thee Midniters |
| *Why Can't We Live Together?* | Timmy Thomas |
| *The Love We Had Stays On My Mind* | The Dells |
| *Be Thankful For What You Got* | William DeVaughn |
| *The World is a Ghetto* | War |
| *It's OK* | The Sunglows |
| *To Be Loved* | Jackie Wilson |
| *The World is a Ghetto* | War |
| *It's OK* | The Sunglows |
| *To Be Loved* | Jackie Wilson |
| *It's OK* | The Sunglows |
| *To Be Loved* | Jackie Wilson |

※

I reach for the dial and discover I can bend the moonlight
by turning the dial on this old radio.
Art Laboe talks to a man who claims to be from Avenal, CA.
It's his little girl's birthday and he's missed a few.
He asks for The Stylistics, you know the one: *You're a Big Girl Now.*

The producer tells Art:
  Nobody is really from Avenal.
The producer reminds Art:
  You know no one is really from Avenal.

I reach for the dial and discover I can bend the moonlight
into a glowing, smiling-now or crying-later crescent,
just as easily, by turning the dial on this old radio.
I'm driving out near San Joaquin because I didn't
know what else to do. A man tells Art Laboe he's lived
in Corcoran for eleven years. Hasn't been out just as long.
He requests a song by the Dramatics. The one about rain.

"So I can remember," the Corcoran man says.
I reach for the dial and discover I can bend the moonlight
so it enters the windows of this car,
through the passenger side, and onto my girl's face.
And damn, she looks fine. We're on the 46
headed to Pismo. Gonna make a fire and
camp out there on the beach. Real romantic like.
A man from Wasco tells Art he's been away so long
his old lady of eight years got a new dude
up in the house, but he's not even trippin.
The Wasco man requests the song *Daddy's Home*
by Shep and the Limelites.

The producer tells Art:
        Art, nobody is *really* from Wasco.
The producer reminds Art:
        Nobody is really from Wasco, Art.
"Art," he says, "you have been misled.
        Art, tell me, why do you insist on
        taking calls from these jokers?"


ART:
*I reached for the dial, long ago, and discovered*
*I could bend moonlight by turning the dial*
*on this old radio. In the proper frequency,*
*the Light reaches towns you and I have never seen*
*Like Wasco*
*Like Avenal*
*Like Corcoran*
*Others*
*Like Kern*
*Like Chino*
*Like Centinela*
*Like Chowchilla.*
*Towns where corporations profit*
*from caged human beings. This light?*
*This light jumps fences. It enters*

*through the thickest of concrete walls.*
*It opens locked iron doors, producer.*
*The light hasn't need for windows.*
*A good Catholic recalls the rule*
*of intercession. I ask: What is a call*
*but a prayer yet to be answered?*
*The caged birds prey and Art intercedes.*
*I carry their plea. I awaken the memories*
*cataloged in the vinyl ridges of each song.*
*I am the needle under the master's hand.*

*ACT IV, SCENE 1*

*CLOVIS. DRIVING. GRAMMA'S LOOKING OUT
THE WINDOW. SHE IS OLDER NOW THAN SHE
WAS YESTERDAY.*

GRAMMA: When you were born, you were supposed to be a girl.

JOSEFO: I know, Gramma.

GRAMMA: They bought everything pink. Everything. I was the only one who got you a boy's blanket. Do you remember that blanket?

JOSEFO: I remember, Gramma.

GRAMMA: I was so happy when you came out a boy.

JOSEFO: Me too, Gramma.

*(Time lapse)*

GRAMMA: Do you see that building there on the corner? That one there?

JOSEFO: Yes, Gramma.

GRAMMA: That used to be an ice-shop. They used to make ice there. In the eighth grade we used to come here because they had a faucet that gave ice water. Ice cold water. There was a man there. I didn't know him. He would come out and mess with us. He would say, "Hey come over here. I got something to show you. Come to the back. I have comething to show you." Of course, none of us went back there. Viejo cochino.

*(Time lapse)*

And when we were at school, the boys used to follow me into the bathroom and get me. I told that one teacher because he would believe me. In those days it was terrible. Nobody believed anything I said. He told me to take my Comadre Rosie. My Comadre Rosie was big. I took my Comadre Rosie with me and when the boys saw my Comadre Rosie, they didn't mess with me anymore. My Comadre Rosie was big and could beat them up.

*(Time lapse)*

Your grandfather told you about the Palomar didn't he? Of course he did. Everybody went to the Palomar. Anyway, me and my comadres were walking home from the Palomar way out on Kearney boulevard and these men pulled up and said they would give us a ride. Well, I looked at my comadres and we said alright on account of our feet hurting so bad. We used to dance the jitterbug. Do you know how to jitterbug? No, that was way before your time. Anyway, this man says, "You'll have to sit on our laps." Carajo. Do you believe that? But we did. We weren't two blocks down the road before those men starting get smart with me and my comadre in the backseat. Hands up my dress and on my legs. Like that. I told him to stop the car. I'll walk, I said. And I got out right there. Me and my comadre Catherine got out. Minerva stayed. She didn't want to walk. I don't know what happened to her. Mensa.

*(Time lapse)*

GRAMMA: Do you still have that blanket?

JOSEFO: No, Gramma.

GRAMMA: It would be all in pieces by now. Your poor mother. She
        had to take all that stuff back. I'm the only one that knew.
        Even the doctor didn't know. But I knew. I'm so happy you
        came out a boy.
JOSEFO: Me too, Gramma.
*Curtain.*

*For Helen "Nan" Ruiz*
*(1926 – 2013)*

# 'SIGUE SIENDO EL REY' OR 'A KING IN LOS ANGELES'

*AFTER RAFAEL CARDENAS*

Don Fausto found his way back to the city
after the drought hit Dinuba real hard.
Since then, he's been chasing work
thru passenger side windows out in
Highland Park. Today he found some
good wages. That's why the vato's so happy.
You can hear 'em from here, all loud.
Or maybe you can't from over there.
I'll tell you, Fausto just let off the pedal some
and he's playing Norteñas from his backpack.
The chain around the gears stays put, but
the bearings still click and the wheels
spin fast as he glides through downtown.
That homie's singing, man, singing for reals.
His tejana hasn't slipped once; I don't know what's
holding it down. No shit, that viejo's singing good too.

*FRESNO, CA*

**PART ONE:**

While driving by Bulldog Lane, you remember Enrique.
He lived on a second floor apartment overlooking Barstow Ave.
Every morning, your father would roll up in truck towing trailer
and beat on the horn until Enrique slid open his window,
threw out a plastic bag with his lunch, crawled half out
and leaped to the ground below. Once up, he'd jump
a six foot fence to get to the truck. Every morning he did this.
But when your father dropped him off at the end of the day,
he'd always leave Enrique at the front door. Neither explained why.

Just then, you remember the day Enrique took a shit
in what was left of the foil he used to wrap his burrito.
He did it in the backyard where the willow tree hung
over the fence and onto the golf course behind each house.
He folded the aluminum neatly and brought the package
to the front and deposited it in the green garbage can.
You and your older brother had a good laugh about it in English.
Enrique just nodded and looked out the window rubbing his forearm
covered in dust and fading black-lined, nearly illegible tattoos.

## PART TWO:

The more important part of the story, you will remember,
occurred the following week when you and your brother went back
to the house. You found the old white lady in some sort of pajama
ensemble, toting a hose pistol with the garbage can on its side.
She looked up at you, her hair already sticking to her face,
breathing heavily through her mouth to communicate her frustration.
As your father's son, and in your best English, you greet her
and ask her what happened. She tells you someone put dog poop
in a foil bag and then put it in her garbage can. After a week
of one hundred degree days, the foil bag burst open and sprayed
the inner walls. The dark matter baked and fumed in the heat.
So there she was, still in her night clothes just before noon, greeting
her gardener's son in slippers stained with Enrique's week old shit.
You're older now. Almost two decades have gone by since that morning
and you can think of no other moment that offered you such satisfaction.

In those days, Enrique moved ten dollar sacks of cheap weed.
He did time. Your father knew. He had done the same.
Everyone's hands were dirty, you say, recognizing the poetic appeal.
You settle on something solid and look up at the corn: It's all true.
One morning, you don't pick up Enrique. You ask your father why
and he tells you the police got him. They chased him near Bulldog Lane.
He barricaded himself in that same apartment he jumped from so many times.
When Enrique refused to come out, the police sent their dog after him.
The dog entered the room where Enrique waited, armed with a kitchen knife.
The animal charged him and he thrust the knife into it's side. The dog
eventually died. You didn't see Enrique ever again. Thinking now, you recall a
story your grandfather told you about restaurants with signs out front that
read, "No dogs or Mexicans allowed." You can't understand why this story
comes to mind. They're not even related, you think to yourself. Not at all.

84

# HIS NAME WAS EFRAIN

*AFTER A PORTRAIT BY SOPHIE RIVERA*

Remember the island left after losing a fight to that horse
with the bat sized cock. It was supposed to be playful.
Loose fists and hoof. Remember the alternating palms
kept open, released beneath muscled haunches, blows
not meant to fall. Recall the animal's rippled ribs expanding
and exhaling shoeless hoofed punches. Coulda walked away.
But what do any of us know about Efrain? The one stoned
behind the wheel of that eight cylinder behemoth rolling
from Jersey with a waistband packed with hidden herb
bound like sausage. Gotta sweat one tail and familiar headlamps.
Shadow figures steer close, itching to drag him to the big show.
He knew what was coming. No sense in belaboring the point.
He already told you. Brother, look at his eyes. He needs no ID.
You're the one just got here. You the one just found out:
there is no sense in rooftops, obits neither. What'r you grabbin at?
You've been misled. Home? No place 'round here, papa.

Some loud morning, you wake:
a hammer sledge meets a black crow-
bar and makes it sing a vibrating,
humming, knuckle-swelling crash
of drum-drum on asphalt black —
note the simple, repeating dashes
painted a cold as fuck yellow,
keeping time under Baldemar's wind-
catching hand, swirling every which way
from the passenger side. See Baldemar
shaking rocks in a paper cup,
sitting there on a plastic milk crate
behind the U-Haul store. He will do what
you want for a square fifteen an hour.
His back, his hands, his limited English,
his supplication, and his silver capped teeth
are yours. When it's over, Baldemar asks
that you return him to where he was found.

Baldemar loves these busted-ass appliances
and the boxes they come in. He pines after them,
spends whole days cruising blocks and alleys
behind other blocks and alleys in search of these
discards. Cardboard is more than a sagging plea
bent against warped walls of grease stained plywood
and cheap stud held tight with splintered twine—
much more to Baldemar's woolen digits breaking
apart plastic casings, removing self-tapping screws,
and small gauge strands like harvested corn husk
or a mat of pubic hair. What's left after removing all
wired components is worth its toil in wrinkled dollars
clasped with two gloved hands dipped in rubber, blue.

Sometimes Baldemar's old lady joins him in the truck.
The streetlamps amplify the phosphorescence of her ponytail.
Nights are for relieving markets of their cartón. Right now,
his vieja's folding and re-placing the gloves Baldemar bought her
because she had trouble fitting into his, large as they were.
He placed the new ones in the middle seat between them.
Without saying a word, she broke the tag, noted the painted S,
then began folding and replacing them on her lap, this way,
then that. Folding them, she replaced one on top of the other till
she knew each glove and could call them by name.

*Brother, I write to you in words only we can understand:*

*Remember when I lit homegirl's album on fire by that canal
and pissed on the ashes? All sad like a punkass. Fuckin
Chuck Taylor All-Star. Backseat footprint n shit. Doggiestyle
n shit, buttass naked with air forces. Rain, fields, the open
backdoor, Smokey coming out the speakers, nighttime lookin
dark as the street. Whole body wet with sheets of cold fukn
water. Both nipples cut glass hard. Each breath a thunder
cloud. Nene never found out. Crazy, man. Hey, remember
those wifebeater tanks down Eighth Street drunk and all
outta fucks? All captain save a hoe in Sanger with the zombie
freak. Spinnin donuts with no headlights, parking break
J turns behind Toys R Us. White boy passed out in the
truckbed switching lanes down 41? Henny and ice like we
knew what was what. Such a gorgeous morning, right? Those
were the days. Cagon might be a crazy ass white boy, but he
had that much right. Those were the days...*

*What I mean to say is: the two of us are gonna lose this old
man. Chai too. The corps and the academy don't mean shit.
Our bullets and poems won't save him. You know. I know. But
'ey, let's smoke a black and point these bitches to the sky and
just pull the fuckin trigger, bro, you know what I'm saying?
You and me, man. Distance and time ain't nothin' but a
thang. I love you. Hasta Pronto*

*Abrazo,*
*JR*

# EPILOGUE

**SAINT PAUL:** (to the Corinthians) Therefore I do not run like a man running aimlessly; I do not fight like a man shadowboxing. No, I beat my body and make it my slave so that after I have preached to others, I myself will not be disqualified for the prize.

ACT V, SCENE 1

WILLIE PERDOMO. HOTEL SHATTUCK PLAZA. BROTHER
THELONIOUS. DON JULIO. SHAKEN. LEMON KNOW LIME.
EYES COLD.

WILLIE: Lorca found his duende in New York. That's all I'm saying.

JOE: At an antique shop, or what?

WILLIE: I'm being serious, Joe. I think the dude found it over on
125<sup>th</sup> Street.

JOE: Ok, ok—like Bobby Womack? I know that song. Wait, no—like
Sinatra.

WILLIE: (Laughs) Nah, Joe. It was the Great Depression. Imagine
bougie ass Lorca walking around there at night. People
dying in the alley, death all around him. It enveloped him
—men transforming into animals right there in the dark
streets—poverty, squalor, alluhdat.

JOE: Yo, imagine a musical number with Lorca crooning like
*Singing in the Rain.* You know, Gene Kelly swinging on a
lamp post and shit—but instead, he's singing something like
*New York, New York...* (Sings) Theeese vagabond shoes are
longing to stray...

WILLIE: You're a fool. I need you to listen up. It's important for this
Josefo character and for your goofy ass, too. See, before
Lorca went out to New York he could go to any bar like this
and listen to any flamenco guitarist doing some wild
unexplainable shit on the strings and, you know, one of
those cats could look Lorca up and down and say, "Nah you
don't got it man."

(To BARTENDER) Yeah, give us another.

(To JOE) The thing of it is, Joe, I mean, when you get down to the nitty gritty realtalk shit, the haunting, terror-black shit—the duende is unmistakable. That's one thing you gotta understand. There's no faking it.

JOE: Like the funk.

WILLIE: The what?

JOE: *The funk.* No fakin' the funk.

WILLIE: Look Fresno boy, it's simple: when Lorca got back, he had the look, you know what I'm saying? He had the look of a man who no longer feared death.

JOE: The eye of the tiger.

WILLIE: Heh, yeah. Eye of the tiger—that's good. You're catching on. You're familiar with bullfighting, right?

JOE: A lil bit. I read alotta Hemingway, for better or worse.

WILLIE: Well, Papa recognized it, but he didn't *have* it, you know what I mean? Imagine the bullfighter, adorned in all sorts of fancy buckles and snaps, embroidery and fine stitching. Tight and sucked up against the body—they weren't big dudes either, some no bigger than a jockey—dancers really, not meant to be brawlers—and they square off against a thousand pounds of pissed-off, rippled muscle, nostril, hoof, and horn. These guys stare that bull right in the face, tame him, and make him tango with nothing more than a fancy throw blanket—spinning veronicas in front of twenty thousand people. Death, man. Dirt. Blood. Death. And Poetry. All of it: fuckin' poetry.

JOE: Damn.

WILLIE: Damn is right, Joe. Damn is right. Now, I gotta ask you...

JOE: What?

WILLIE: Which one are you? The bullfighter or the bull?

JOE: [Pause] Well...I dunno.

WILLIE: You better know.

JOE: I don't know, Willie.

WILLIE: Which one is Josefo?

*Curtain.*

"Baldemar's Jale II" and "Baldemar's Jale III" appeared in
    *Southern Humanities Review*
"Josefo Chats with Chewy" appeared in *Acentos Review*
"Southpaw Curse" appeared in *Huizache*
"Going the Distance" and "Think About the Fight" appeared in
    *Flies Cockroaches and Poets*
"Shadowboxing" appears in *Canto*
"Boy Scout Training" and "They Don't Remember You, They
    Remember the Rep" appeared in *bozalta*
"Sigue Siendo El Rey or A King in Los Angeles" appeared in
    MAS ACA by Rafael Cardenas


Thank you to my Grandmother, Helen Ruiz, who was the first to
nurture my writing. Thank you, Gramma, for showing me how to
tell a good story. Thank you to my Mother and Grandfather for a
lifetime of faith and for driving and flying to all the poetry readings.

For my late father, Paul Andres Rios. By the time this book arrives,
it will have been 15 years since your death. You would be 62. Thank
you for the lessons and the work. Thank you for showing a ten-year-
old how to drive a Bobcat.

Thank you Javier Huerta, Leon Salvatierra, Maceo Montoya, and
Lisa Marie Rollins for being my family in the Bay. Thank you
Ishmael Armendariz. We didn't always keep the lights on, but we
found food and were never evicted. Thank you Suzy Huerta for
four years of love and care in life and in poetry. Thank you Carissa
Garcia for coming through in any city and for all these years. Thank
you Stephany Cuevas for being an advocate for me in these streets
and my most trusted critic behind closed doors. Thank you Adrian
Schurr for being smooth af and for being a rock in times of need.
Thank you Malaquias and Lezlie Montoya for welcoming me into
your home and into your family. Thanks Lye for your friendship and
for putting me up in your houses all over the place and showing me

a world of art outside of the one I knew. Thank you Jennifer Mora for supporting and pushing me, always.

Thank you Professors Genaro Padilla and Marcial Gonzalez for always checking up on me while at Berkeley. You created a world where a young Chicano English major could see himself in books. Thank you Willie Perdomo for seeing my vision for this collection before I could and thank you for asking the questions that eventually got me here. Thank you Francisco Aragon for sending me out to Red Wing, MN to finish this manuscript. Thank you Robert Hedin for the quiet care you paid me while I stayed in your grandfather's house.

Thank you Michele Serros. Thank you Francisco X. Alarcon. Thank you Victor Martinez. Thank you Jose Montoya. Thank you Luis Omar Salinas. Thank you Larry Levis. Thank you Ernesto Trejo. Thank you Andres Montoya. Thank you Tomas Rivera. Thank you Octavio Romano. Thank you Alfred Arteaga. You expanded this territory so I can roam free.

Thank you Fresno writing community: Lee Herrick, Dympna Ugwu-Oju, Tim Z Hernandez, Teresa Navarro Tarazi, Juan Luis Guzman, Sara Borjas, Cynthia Guardado, David Campos, Anthony Cody, Soul Vang, Mia Barraza, Marisol Baca, Michael Medrano, Bryan Medina and many others.

Lupe Manriquez, Melissa Chinchilla, Teresa Flores, Mariela Nevarez, Luis Guizar, Pete Galindo, Rafael Cardenas, Greg Orloff, Abel Salas, Luivette Resto, Daisy Cuevas, Liliana Hernandez, Javier Zamora, Laurie Ann Guerrero, Reyna Grande, Yajaira Salvatierra, Norma Liliana Valdez, Oscar Bermeo, Barbara Jane Reyes, Sandra Garcia Rivera, Lucha Corpi, Harold Terezon, Macondo, VONA, the Anderson Center, the staff at *bozalta*—thank you all for giving to the community that supports me and my work. Couldn't have written this without you and many others. c/s

Joseph Rios was born in Clovis, CA. Joseph's work has appeared in: *Los Angeles Review, Huizache, New Border, Southern Humanities Review, Poets Responding to SB1070,* and *bozalta.* He is a recipient of the John K. Walsh residency fellowship from Notre Dame. Joseph is a VONA alumnus, a Macondo fellow, and a graduate of the University of California, Berkeley. He lives in Los Angeles.

*Shadowboxing: poems and impersonations*
by Joseph Rios

Cover Image: David Rathman, Untitled,
ink and watercolor on canvas, 30 x 36 inches, 2009

Cover and interior set in Hypatia Sans Pro and Electra LT Std

Cover and interior design by Gillian Olivia Blythe Hamel

Offset printed in the United States
by Sheridan Books, Chelsea, Michigan
On 55# Glatfelter B19 Antique
Acid Free Archival Quality Recycled Paper

Publication of this book was made possible in part by gifts from:
The Clorox Company
The New Place Fund
Robin & Curt Caton

Omnidawn Publishing
Oakland, California
2017
Rusty Morrison & Ken Keegan, senior editors & co-publishers
Gillian Olivia Blythe Hamel, managing editor
Cassandra Smith, poetry editor & book designer
Sharon Zetter, poetry editor, book designer & development officer
Avren Keating, poetry editor, fiction editor & marketing assistant
Liza Flum, poetry editor
Juliana Paslay, fiction editor
Gail Aronson, fiction editor
Trisha Peck, marketing assistant
Cameron Stuart, marketing assistant
Natalia Cinco, marketing assistant
Maria Kosiyanenko, marketing assistant
Emma Thomason, administrative assistant
SD Sumner, copyeditor
Kevin Peters, *OmniVerse* Lit Scene editor
Sara Burant, *OmniVerse* reviews editor